CHARLES DARWIN
DEVELOPS THE THEORY
OF EVOLUTION

by Douglas Hustad

Content Consultant
Stephen C. Burnett, PhD
Professor of Biology
Department of Natural Sciences
Clayton State University

Core Library

An Imprint of Abdo Publishing
abdopublishing.com

abdopublishing.com

Published by Abdo Publishing, a division of ABDO, PO Box 398166, Minneapolis, Minnesota 55439. Copyright © 2016 by Abdo Consulting Group, Inc. International copyrights reserved in all countries. No part of this book may be reproduced in any form without written permission from the publisher. Core Library™ is a trademark and logo of Abdo Publishing.

Printed in the United States of America, North Mankato, Minnesota
092015
012016

THIS BOOK CONTAINS
RECYCLED MATERIALS

Cover Photo: Bettmann/Corbis/AP Images
Interior Photos: Bettmann/Corbis/AP Images, 1; Aleksander Mirski/iStockphoto, 4; Bettmann/Corbis, 6; Paul D. Stewart/Science Source, 9, 16; Science Source, 12, 26, 39 (bottom); DEA Picture Library/Getty Images, 18, 45; Royal Astronomical Society/Science Source, 21; Dorling Kindersley/Thinkstock, 23; Mario Tama/Getty Images, 28; Mary Martin/Science Source, 30; Armando Garcia/Science Source, 36; David Gifford/Science Source, 39 (top)

Editor: Arnold Ringstad
Series Designer: Maggie Villaume

Library of Congress Control Number: 2015945847

Cataloging-in-Publication Data
Hustad, Douglas.
 Charles Darwin develops the theory of evolution / Douglas Hustad.
   p. cm. -- (Great moments in science)
ISBN 978-1-68078-015-4 (lib. bdg.)
Includes bibliographical references and index.
1. Naturalists--England--Juvenile literature. 2. Evolution (Biology)--Juvenile literature.   I. Title.
576.8--dc23
                                                    2015945847

CONTENTS

ISLANDS OF EVIDENCE

When the crew of the HMS *Beagle* spotted land on September 15, 1835, they had already seen amazing wonders. After departing from England in 1831, they had sailed around all of South America. Now, with the Galapagos Islands in view, there were even greater discoveries to come. There was history to be made.

Exciting scientific discoveries lay ahead as the *Beagle* approached the Galapagos Islands.

Darwin studied a wide variety of plants and animals in the Galapagos Islands.

The ship's scientist, Charles Darwin, had made thousands of observations. He had gathered many samples. He had studied plants and animals throughout the journey. But it was his work in the Galapagos Islands that would make him famous.

Darwin collected several kinds of finches in the Galapagos Islands. These birds had beaks of different shapes and sizes. He did not attach any meaning to this. He did not even take the time to label which island each bird came from. He knew wildlife varied from island to island even though they were all close together. But he did not yet consider it significant.

Darwin's Finches

Darwin returned home from his voyage on October 2, 1836. He spent a few months organizing his collection and writing. In early 1837, he brought the finches to the Zoological Society in London, England. They would be in good hands.

PERSPECTIVES
Sir Charles Lyell

Charles Lyell was a highly regarded geologist in the 1800s. He was one of the world's most prominent naturalists at the time of Darwin's voyage on the *Beagle*. Lyell's *Principles of Geology Vol. 1* was a great influence on Darwin. He used it as a guide in collecting samples and making observations. Darwin met Lyell shortly after his return to England. The two became friends. Lyell did not accept evolution until the 1860s. Still, Lyell encouraged Darwin to publish his work on the subject. Darwin later published his own books about geology. He felt he owed so much to Lyell that his knowledge of geology came "half out of Lyell's brain."

The society's ornithologist, John Gould, spent months studying them.

Darwin came to visit Gould in March. Darwin had recently moved to London to be closer to the work being done on his specimens. Gould had made some amazing discoveries. The samples did not represent many different types of birds. Instead, they were all closely related to each other. Plus, 25 of the 26 bird species Darwin brought back were completely new species. They were found nowhere else in the world.

Darwin was astonished at the findings. It was a very exciting mystery. How had so many new species arisen on this small group of islands? To investigate, Darwin needed to know which island each bird came from. He had not kept good notes. He hoped others might have. He reached out to other crewmembers of the *Beagle* to try to put the pieces together.

The "B" Notebook

Luckily, Darwin got help from the crew. He determined where each bird came from.

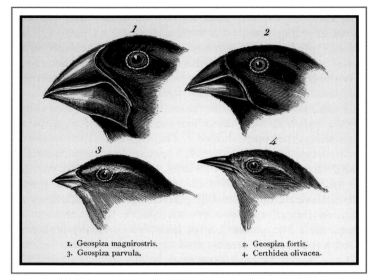

Thinking about the variety of beak types on the Galapagos finches helped Darwin reach important conclusions about evolution.

1. Geospiza magnirostris.
2. Geospiza fortis.
3. Geospiza parvula.
4. Certhidea olivacea.

He discovered that different species lived on different islands. Each was well suited to its environment. One major difference between them could be seen in their beaks. Some had different shapes to suit the kind of food they ate. Some that ate insects had larger beaks. Others that mainly ate seeds off the ground had smaller beaks.

Darwin wondered how the different species came to be. In July 1837, he began his "B" notebook. In it, he considered the possibility of transmutation. This was the changing of one species into another over time. Transmutation would later be called evolution.

In the Galapagos, it seemed one original finch species had been scattered across several islands. On each island, the survival of the birds best suited to the new environment eventually led to a distinct species.

On one page of the notebook, Darwin made a sketch. It was a tree with branches on it. It was the first representation of how all life on Earth is related. One species, the tree's trunk, could become many different species, the branches. At the top of the page, Darwin wrote,

"I think." It was still just an idea. Darwin kept it secret. It would take decades more research until he was ready to share his theory with the world.

FURTHER EVIDENCE

Chapter One discusses Darwin's study of the Galapagos finches. What was one of the main points of this chapter? What key evidence supports this point? Find a quote at the website below that supports the main point. Does the quote support an existing piece of evidence? Does it offer new evidence?

The Significance of the Finches

mycorelibrary.com/evolution

CHAPTER TWO

A REMARKABLE UPBRINGING

Charles Robert Darwin was born on February 12, 1809, in Shrewsbury, England. Scientific interests ran in his family. His grandfather, Erasmus Darwin, was a doctor and was very interested in the world around him. Years before Charles was born, Erasmus wrote a book about the origin of life on Earth. These interests were picked up by his son, Charles's father.

As a child, Charles, left, was interested in nature.

Charles's father was also a doctor. He encouraged his son to go into medicine. But Charles was more interested in other things, such as collecting bugs. He and his brother, also named Erasmus, loved doing chemistry experiments in the family's garden shed. Charles made more time for hunting animals and riding horses than studying.

When Charles performed poorly in school, his father pulled him out. Charles worked as his father's assistant. This medical training allowed him to go to Edinburgh University in 1825 and train to be a doctor.

Shifting Interests

But Charles was not well suited to a career in medicine. He was bored studying it. And he could not bear to watch surgery being performed. He pursued his other interests. He liked to talk to local fishermen and see the different fish they caught each day. He met with naturalists and learned about their theories.

Darwin eventually left medical school. He went to the University of Cambridge in 1828 to become a minister. Charles was not particularly religious. But being a country pastor would give him a lot of free time to study science. This was what appealed to Charles most.

At Cambridge

Charles enjoyed life at Cambridge. But he still was not a great student. His ministerial studies did not interest him. However, the environment of Cambridge was rich with all that Charles loved. He met many fellow students who shared his interests. And he had access to some of the best minds of science in the world.

One man who would be a great influence on Charles was John Stevens Henslow. He was a botany

Darwin's Religion

Darwin set himself on the path to the ministry out of convenience. He was not completely comfortable joining the Church of England. But he felt it would fit his lifestyle as a naturalist. Darwin did not come from a religious background. His father, grandfather, and brother were all freethinkers. That means they did not align themselves with a particular set of beliefs. This was unusual at the time.

Henslow helped inspire Darwin's interest in pursuing scientific study.

lecturer at Cambridge. Charles frequently attended his classes and admired his work. Henslow recognized Charles as a special student. They frequently had discussions and went on walks together. Charles became known around Cambridge as "the man who walks with Henslow."

Henslow was also a minister. Charles believed he would follow the exact same path. But as he read more and more on natural science, his intentions changed. He dreamed of exploring the world. Henslow encouraged Charles to follow these dreams.

In 1831 Charles arrived home to find a letter from Henslow. The minister had recommended him for a voyage around the world. The HMS *Beagle* would be conducting a two-year mapping of South America. Charles had the opportunity to be the ship's naturalist. He accepted the offer.

PERSPECTIVES
John Stevens Henslow

Henslow may have seen some of himself in Charles. He also was interested in nature from a young age. He became a professor of botany at Cambridge in 1825. He held the post until his death in 1861. Henslow's teaching style was very different from that of many of his peers. He encouraged students to get out of the classroom and observe the world. He also hosted them in his home for discussions over dinner. Henslow had a great impact on both Charles's personal and professional life. Later in life, Charles and his wife even named three of their children, Annie, George, and Leonard, after Henslow's children.

THE VOYAGE OF THE *BEAGLE*

Henslow believed Darwin was the most qualified person for the job of naturalist aboard the *Beagle*. The ship's captain, Robert FitzRoy, wanted a naturalist on board the ship to take samples and make observations. The main purpose of the voyage was mapping. But it was also a chance to see new plants and animals.

The *Beagle* was large and sturdy enough to sail around the entire planet.

Days passed before Darwin was able to accept the position. He argued with his father about whether he would go. Finally, Darwin went to London to speak with FitzRoy. The captain had already offered the job to someone else. Luckily for Darwin that offer had been declined. Darwin was in.

The crew of the *Beagle* had planned to set sail on October 10, 1831. After several delays, the ship finally left port on December 27. Darwin was not used to life at sea. He got seasick quickly and often. He spent as much time on land as possible when the ship stopped. When he was not too ill, he collected samples.

Early Discoveries

Throughout the ship's first year at sea, Darwin made some remarkable discoveries. While in the Cape Verde Islands off the western coast of Africa, he noticed a line of white shells in a rock face. The shells were 45 feet (14 m) above the water. He reasoned that the land must constantly be shifting. That line of shells was once underwater.

In the decades after the voyage of the *Beagle*, FitzRoy became a meteorologist and the governor of New Zealand.

Around August 1832, Darwin began to find a lot of fossils while in South America. He did not know much about them. But he figured they might be important. Captain FitzRoy scolded Darwin for bringing too much "useless junk" on board.

But one of Darwin's fossil collections was very important. He discovered the skeleton of a long-extinct giant sloth. Only one complete skeleton of this animal was known to exist in the world at the time. Extinction was not a concept that was well understood. Captain FitzRoy, like many other religious people of his time, believed animals became extinct when they could not fit on Noah's Ark.

Darwin began to connect the samples he found with the history of Earth. He noted that some fossils were found with seashells, as if water had once covered them. After an earthquake in Chile, he saw how the land had risen. This led him to believe South America

PERSPECTIVES
Captain Robert FitzRoy

The captain of the *Beagle* was interested in natural science. He wanted someone knowledgeable and well trained to serve on his ship. He also wanted somebody with whom he could talk. Darwin was well suited for the position. FitzRoy and Darwin got along well and sometimes had dinner together. Later, Darwin's views on evolution caused some disagreement. FitzRoy disagreed with Darwin's theory of evolution for religious reasons. He thought people should believe the Bible above the word of any man.

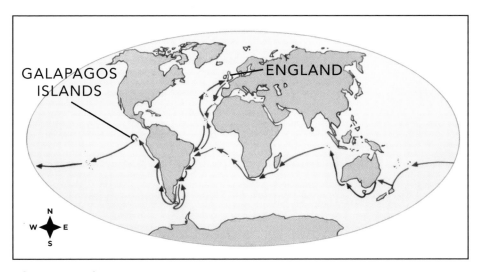

The *Beagle's* Voyage
The map above shows the route of Darwin's voyage on the HMS *Beagle*. This voyage took him all around the world and lasted nearly five years. Why do you think the ship's crew chose this route?

was rising over time. He concluded Earth must be quite old.

The Galapagos Islands

Shortly before arriving at the Galapagos Islands in September 1835, Darwin wrote a letter home to his sister. He said he was looking forward to seeing the islands. He believed they would have fascinating animals and natural features to study. Over the next several weeks, he would be proven right.

The Galapagos are a chain of islands off the west coast of South America. The name is Spanish for "tortoise." The islands are famous for their giant tortoises. Darwin learned from locals that the tortoises varied from island to island. This was also the case for the finches and other birds that Darwin collected.

On October 20, 1835, the *Beagle* left the Galapagos. It set sail for Tahiti, which is more than 3,000 miles (4,828 km) away.

The Voyage Ends

The *Beagle* sailed to Tahiti, New Zealand, and Australia. When the *Beagle* arrived at ports, it offloaded some of Darwin's samples and notes. These items were

The Fate of the *Beagle*

Darwin's voyage was one of three made by the *Beagle* on surveying trips. The ship made similar voyages from 1826–1830 and 1837–1843. Following its third voyage, the ship was no longer in good sailing condition. It was anchored in place on the Thames River as a watch ship. By 1863 it was used as housing for members of the coast guard. In 1870 it was sold for scrap and broken up.

sent back to England. The *Beagle*'s route then took it through the Indian Ocean. From there, the ship went around Africa before returning home.

Darwin received a letter from his sister just a few months before returning. She informed him that Henslow had been distributing his letters and samples in England. Darwin was already a celebrity.

The voyage was supposed to last two years. But by the time the *Beagle* landed in England on October 2, 1836, it had been gone for nearly five years.

EXPLORE ONLINE

Chapter Three discusses Charles Darwin's voyage on the HMS *Beagle*. The website below goes more in depth on some of the other things Darwin saw on his journey. How is the information on the website different than the information in Chapter Three? What new information did you learn from the website?

The Rest of the Voyage

mycorelibrary.com/evolution

CHAPTER FOUR

EARLY RESEARCH IN LONDON

As soon as the *Beagle* docked in England, Darwin headed home to see his family. Over the next few weeks, he caught up with his brother, Erasmus. He also spent time with Henslow. He worked on cataloguing the thousands of specimens he brought back from the voyage.

On January 4, 1837, Darwin made a speech to the Royal Geological Society of London. He talked

Once Darwin arrived home, he began the difficult work of making sense of all he had seen on the voyage of the *Beagle*.

Darwin's "B" notebook featured his earliest tree diagram of evolution.

about his observations of the earthquake in Chile. He suggested that since Earth is always changing, animals change with it. This was a new theory. Most people believed that animals did not change. Old species simply went extinct and new species replaced them. But Darwin's speech was well received.

Darwin spent much of 1837 pondering evolution. In May 1837, he first thought of monkeys as a human ancestor. In filling his "B" notebook, Darwin asked himself some questions. Was there evidence for evolution? How did animal species adapt to their environments? How did they form? And what was the explanation for different species having similarities?

But Darwin only discussed these concepts with one person. His brother was like-minded, and they shared ideas. Darwin could not talk about evolution with anyone else. The topic was controversial. But Darwin would not keep it a secret forever.

Evolutionary Thought at the Time

The origin of the human species had been considered for centuries before Darwin. He was not the first to believe all life on Earth evolved. But he was the first to describe exactly how it worked.

Some ancient Greek philosophers had ideas about evolution too. Aristotle had his own model. He believed species never changed. He attempted to classify all known animals. Carolus Linnaeus did the same approximately 2,000 years later. The Swedish naturalist's system of classification is still in use today. He believed in an evolutionary system, but he thought it was directed by a higher power.

Darwin's grandfather Erasmus was a well-known doctor, inventor, and poet.

This was the popular belief at the time. People did not believe life could descend from a common ancestor. They thought Earth was very young, only about 6,000 years old. People also believed humans were not part of the same system as animals. They thought humans were created separately.

People started to challenge this view before Darwin. Darwin's own grandfather had written a book on the origin of life. However, he had little evidence to support his theories. Darwin had collected a tremendous amount of evidence on his journey aboard the *Beagle*. He now needed to sort through it to strengthen his theory. Then he would be ready to present the theory of evolution to the world.

The Formation of a Theory

Because Darwin was not ready to publish his theories, he had to be creative. He reached out to animal breeders for information. Without revealing his thoughts on evolution, he asked questions about how they bred animals. This gave him information on how species form and develop. But there was a limit to how much the breeders knew. Some of his questions were too complex for them.

Darwin published his diary of the *Beagle* voyage in 1839. He also finished his notebooks of research on evolution. At the same time, his health was growing worse. By 1842 he moved out of London. He and his family moved to the country, where Darwin continued working in peace.

Darwin was struggling with the reasons species changed and adapted. One day it came to him while he was out riding a horse. The individuals that developed useful traits survived. Because these individuals survived and were able to have offspring, they passed those useful traits down to the next generation. This results in adaptations over time, and it can eventually lead to species becoming new species. On the Galapagos Islands, the finches that developed the beaks best suited for food were the ones that survived. They then passed their traits on to their offspring, and these traits spread through the population. Darwin called this process natural selection.

In 1844, for the first time, Darwin shared the full extent of his theories. He told his friend Joseph Dalton Hooker. Hooker surprised Darwin by not rejecting the idea right away. He asked to hear more. Darwin was thrilled with this encouragement. He kept working. Hooker became his assistant.

The Origin of *Origin*

In 1856 Darwin received a 20-page paper in the mail. It was by a naturalist named Alfred Russel Wallace. The paper was about evolution. Wallace's work was similar to Darwin's. Darwin was not impressed with the paper. His friend Charles Lyell encouraged Darwin to publish his own findings.

Darwin set to work expanding on his writings. On July 1, 1858, papers by both Darwin and Wallace were read to the Linnean Society, a scientific group in London. The reaction was mixed. Darwin's ideas

PERSPECTIVES
Alfred Russel Wallace

Like Darwin, Wallace developed his theories by observing the world. He had been to South America. He noticed differences in specimens and came to similar conclusions as Darwin. But they had disagreements. Wallace believed evolution had a goal. He felt it was striving to make the perfect man. Darwin did not see it this way. Though they worked on similar things, the men were not rivals. Later in life, Darwin arranged for a pension for Wallace from the government.

Darwin's Barnacle Research

In addition to his evolution research, Darwin was consumed by another project. For eight years, he studied tiny sea creatures called barnacles. His work focused mainly on cataloguing them and studying the differences between them. This work brought him respect from the scientific community.

were revolutionary and conflicted with many people's religious beliefs. If species simply changed into other species, some people believed this left no room for a creator.

Darwin continued working on a book-length description of his theories. He wanted to provide an overview of the ideas and evidence he had gathered so far. Darwin finished it in March 1859. His book *On the Origin of Species* was published on November 24, 1859.

Despite doing a lot of the same research, Wallace and Darwin were not enemies. In 1860 Wallace outlined his praise for Darwin:

> I know not how, or to whom, to express fully my admiration of Darwin's book. To him it would seem flattery, to others self-praise; but I do honestly believe that with however much patience I had worked and experimented on the subject, I could never have approached the completeness of his book, its vast accumulation of evidence, its overwhelming argument, and its admirable tone and spirit. I really feel thankful that it has not been left to me to give the theory to the world. Mr. Darwin has created a new science and a new philosophy; and I believe that never has such a complete illustration of a new branch of human knowledge been due to the labours and researches of a single man.

Source: Tim M. Berra. *Charles Darwin: The Concise Story of an Extraordinary Man.* Baltimore, MD: Johns Hopkins University Press, 2008. Print. 66.

Point of View

Wallace has a very high opinion of Darwin. Why do you think he was glad it was Darwin who published the theory of evolution, and not him? Do you agree Darwin was best for the job?

ON

THE ORIGIN OF SPECIES

BY MEANS OF NATURAL SELECTION,

OR THE

PRESERVATION OF FAVOURED RACES IN THE STRUGGLE
FOR LIFE.

By CHARLES DARWIN, M.A.,

FELLOW OF THE ROYAL, GEOLOGICAL, LINNÆAN, ETC., SOCIETIES;
AUTHOR OF 'JOURNAL OF RESEARCHES DURING H. M. S. BEAGLE'S VOYAGE
ROUND THE WORLD.'

LONDON:

JOHN MURRAY, ALBEMARLE STREET.

1859.

CHAPTER FIVE

PUBLICATION OF ON THE ORIGIN OF SPECIES

rigin was an immediate success. Its first 1,500 copies sold out right away. A second edition of 3,000 copies was printed quickly. The book caused quite a stir. Some felt the book led people away from Christianity.

Darwin did not have to deal with much of the controversy himself. His home out in the country kept him away from it all. Darwin knew his work would be

On the Origin of Species sparked a major controversy upon its publication in 1859.

Bishop Samuel Wilberforce

Wilberforce was a prominent religious figure when *On the Origin of Species* came out. He helped convince Queen Victoria not to knight Darwin in 1859. In an 1860 debate, Wilberforce spent a half hour criticizing the book. Thomas Huxley represented Darwin at the debate. Wilberforce even asked Huxley whether he was descended from apes on his mother's or father's side. This entertained the crowd but enraged Huxley. Other antievolutionists were also in attendance. One was the captain of the *Beagle*, Robert FitzRoy. He held a Bible in the air and urged the audience to believe its words, rather than a man's.

controversial. He even addressed the controversy in the book. He did not ignore religion. He pointed out how natural selection was more likely than creation.

Some people accepted the new theory. The book mostly got good reviews. Even Queen Victoria's royal family seemed to enjoy it. Darwin was hurt by the critical reviews, but they did not harm his reputation. Through his life, he edited five editions

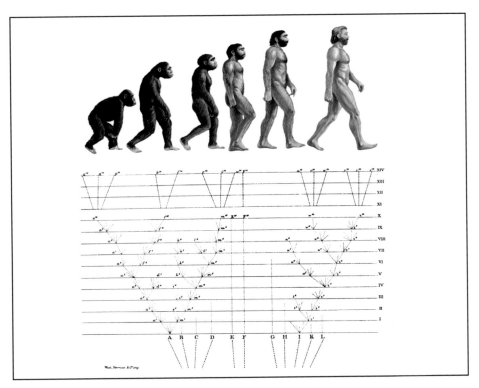

Depicting Evolution
On top is a common depiction of the evolution of humans over time. Below it is a sketch made by Darwin showing how species evolve. How do these visual demonstrations of evolution differ? Which one tells a more accurate and complete story of how evolution works?

of the book. *Origin* made him one of the world's most famous scientists.

After this success, Darwin prepared to tell the next part of the story. In *Origin*, Darwin did not address the evolution of man. This would be the focus of his new project.

The Descent of Man and Later Life

The first time Darwin used the word *evolution* in its modern sense was in *The Descent of Man*. This book came out in 1871. In it Darwin applied his theories from *Origin* to humans.

Descent was a great success. It produced less controversy than *On the Origin of Species*. After publishing it, Darwin stopped his work on evolution, though he continued to make observations about plants and animals.

Darwin's health continued to worsen. He died on April 19, 1882. He was buried near Sir Isaac Newton, another one of the greatest scientists of all time.

Darwin wrote in his book about how species adapted to fit their environment. The following passage is from Chapter III of *On the Origin of Species*:

> How have all those exquisite adaptations of one part of the organisation to another part, and to the conditions of life, and of one distinct organic being to another being, been perfected? We see these beautiful co-adaptations most plainly in the woodpecker and missletoe; and only a little less plainly in the humblest parasite which clings to the hairs of a quadruped or feather of a bird; in the structure of the beetle which dives through the water; in the plumed seed which is wafted by the gentlest breeze; in short, we see beautiful adaptation everywhere and in every part of the organic world.

Source: Charles Darwin. The Annotated Origin. Cambridge, MA: Harvard, 2009. Print. 30.

What's the Big Idea?

Take a close look at this passage. What is the connection between the examples Darwin cites and the idea of adaptation? How have these species' adaptations enabled them to thrive?

IMPORTANT DATES

1809

Darwin is born in Shrewsbury, England.

1825

Darwin attends Edinburgh University to train to be a doctor.

1828

Darwin attends Cambridge to train for the ministry.

1837

Darwin makes the "tree of life" sketch in his "B" notebook.

1839

Darwin publishes his diary of the Beagle voyage.

1856

After reading of Alfred Russel Wallace's research into evolution, Darwin begins to put together his ideas for publication.

1831

Darwin sets sail on the HMS *Beagle* as the ship's naturalist.

1835

The *Beagle* surveys the Galapagos Islands.

1836

The *Beagle* lands in England after a nearly five-year journey.

1859

Darwin's book *On the Origin of Species* is published.

1871

Darwin's book *The Descent of Man* is published.

1882

Darwin dies on April 19.

STOP AND THINK

Tell the Tale

Chapters One and Three of this book discuss Darwin's time in the Galapagos Islands. Imagine you are taking a similar journey. Write 200 words about the creatures you see on your trip. What would you want to observe about each one?

Surprise Me

Chapter Two discusses Darwin's early life and education. After reading this book, what two or three facts about this part of Darwin's life did you find most surprising? Write a few sentences about each fact. Why did you find each fact surprising?

Dig Deeper

After reading this book, what questions do you still have about evolution? With an adult's help, find a few reliable sources that can help you answer your questions. Write a paragraph about what you learned.

Why Do I Care?

Humans evolved just like all animals on Earth. But some of our adaptations are harder to see than an animal's. What do you think are some adaptations that humans have made? How do they make us suited for life in our environment?

GLOSSARY

ancestor
a plant or animal from which another plant or animal is descended

botany
the study of plants

controversial
resulting in public arguments

extinct
when a whole species of animal is gone from Earth

geologist
a person who studies rocks and the earth

naturalist
a person who studies natural history

ornithologist
a person who studies birds

pension
an amount of money paid to someone on a regular basis, usually by the government or a past employer

species
a specific type of animal

specimen
a sample of a plant or animal taken for study

survey
a study of the size and shape of land for mapping purposes

LEARN MORE

Books

Lasky, Kathryn. *One Beetle Too Many: The Extraordinary Adventures of Charles Darwin.* Cambridge, MA: Candlewick Press, 2014.

Pringle, Laurence. *Billions of Years, Amazing Changes: The Story of Evolution.* Honesdale, PA: Boyds Mills, 2011.

Websites

To learn more about Great Moments in Science, visit **booklinks.abdopublishing.com**. These links are routinely monitored and updated to provide the most current information available.

Visit **mycorelibrary.com** for free additional tools for teachers and students.

INDEX

ABOUT THE AUTHOR

Douglas Hustad is a children's author from Minnesota. He has written several books on science topics for young people.